Table of contents

Foreword

Welcome to the IT Infrastructure Library module on ***Software Control & Distribution.***

In their respective subject areas, the IT Infrastructure Library publications complement and provide more detail than the IS Guides.

The ethos behind the development of the IT Infrastructure Library is the recognition that organizations are becoming increasingly dependent on IT in order to satisfy their corporate aims and meet their business needs. This growing dependency leads to a growing requirement for high-quality IT services. In this context quality means matched to business needs and user requirements as these evolve.

This module is one of a series of codes of practice intended to facilitate the quality management of IT Services, and of the IT Infrastructure. (By IT Infrastructure, we mean organizations' computers and networks - hardware, software and computer-related telecommunications, upon which applications systems and IT services are built and run). The codes of practice are intended to assist organizations to provide quality IT service in the face of skill shortages, system complexity, rapid change, current and future user requirements, growing user expectations, etc.

Underpinning the IT Infrastructure is the Environmental Infrastructure upon which it is built. Environmental topics are covered in a separate set of guides within the IT Infrastructure Library.

IT Infrastructure Management is a complex subject which for presentational and practical reasons has been broken down within the IT Infrastructure Library into a series of modules. A complete list of current and planned modules is available from the CCTA IT Infrastructure Management Services at the address given at the back of this module.

The structure of this module is in essence :

* *a Management summary aimed at senior IT managers (Directors of IT and above) and some "senior customers"; (typically Civil Service grades 3 - 7)*

* *the main body of the text aimed at IT middle management (typically grades 7 to HEO).*

*The module gives the main **guidance** in sections 3 to 5; explains the **benefits, costs and possible problems** in section 6, which may be of interest to senior staff; and provides information on **tools** (requirements and examples of real-life availability) in section 7.*

CCTA is working with the IT industry to foster the development of software tools to underpin the guidance contained within the codes of practice (ie to make adherence to the module more practicable), and ultimately to automate functions.

If you have any comments on this or other modules, do please let us know. A comment sheet is provided with every module; please feel free to photocopy the comment sheet or to let us have your views via any other medium.

Thank you. We hope you find this module useful.

1. Management summary

Introduction

Every business organization must safeguard and manage its assets, especially if they are vital to the running of the organization's businesses.

All too often computer software, perhaps because of its somewhat intangible nature, is not regarded as a true asset and is therefore not properly controlled. Yet software can be an extremely valuable asset, which has a marked effect on the efficiency and effectiveness of organizations' businesses. The control of software is of paramount importance to most organizations.

Software can be copied, transmitted to other computers and modified easily by those who have access to the necessary facilities. Current trends towards distributed IT systems mean that multiple copies of the same software item are issued to remote locations, often into the hands of users. It is essential to the smooth and economic running of an organization's IT services (and of their businesses as a whole) that these processes are controlled.

By purchasing software, organizations acquire rights and obligations (for example maintenance rights, obligations not to make copies). Software control is needed for organizations to make best use of their rights and to honour their obligations.

What is SC&D?

A software control and distribution (SC&D) function, as covered in this module, is responsible for:

* the storage of management-authorized software in both centralized and distributed systems

* the release of the software into the live environment

* distribution of the software to remote locations

* implementation (bringing into service) of the software.

The main types of software to be controlled are application programs developed in-house, bought-in application and utility software, supplier-provided systems software and personal computer (PC) software packages. All software needs to be managed effectively from development/ purchase through testing to the live environment.

This module

The module outlines how to plan, implement and run a SC&D function and describes the support tools that will be required. It also describes the key people involved and their roles. A job description for the SC&D Manager is provided at Annex B.

The module describes the important interfaces to the configuration management and change management functions, without which it is not possible efficiently and effectively to control, store, distribute and implement software.

Finally...

Although there are costs associated with implementing SC&D, these are far less than the potential costs of not adequately controlling software. Increasing cases of damage due to software viruses support this view.

Because of the importance of SC&D, all organizations should implement a SC&D function as quickly as possible. To start with, the function should be applied to newly developed or newly purchased software.

2. Introduction

2.1 Purpose

The purpose of this module is to provide guidance to organizations on the procedures needed to plan for, implement, run and audit an SC&D function. The module also gives advice on how to justify such a function.

2.2 Target readership

This module is aimed at IT services managers and SC&D managers and their staff. It will also be of interest to Change, Configuration, Problem, Security and Help Desk Managers and their staff, to applications development personnel, and to staff responsible for the operational acceptance testing of software.

2.3 Scope

Software control and distribution (SC&D) is part of configuration management. Configuration management records, in a configuration management database (CMDB), the content and context of an IT infrastructure, including software items, and documents changes planned and implemented to the infrastructure. SC&D is responsible, under or within configuration management, for the physical storage, distribution, and implementation of software items. SC&D ensures that only correctly released and currently authorized versions of software are actually brought into use.

To fulfil these responsibilities, SC&D as described in this module uses a Definitive Software Library and carries out the processes of release build, distribution and implementation:

* **Definitive Software Library (DSL)** - this is a secure software library where all versions of software configuration items (CIs) that have been accepted from the developer or supplier are held in their definitive, quality-controlled form (the DSL is a logical library which may, by necessity, have to occupy more than one physical location)

* **Release Build** - this is a set of processes whereby a software release is built from items in the DSL, selected by reference to the CMDB

3

* **Distribution** - this is the process of copying the releases from the build environment into test and, later, live environments. These live environments may be widely distributed

* **Implementation** - this is the process of bringing the software into live use at the target locations.

Note - a software release is a set of new and/or changed CIs which are tested and introduced into the live environment together. In most circumstances a release will also include documentation, and in some instances hardware is included too.

Although software that is developed in-house has to be controlled throughout the application life-cycle, this module concentrates on the controls necessary from the point of handover from the applications development team to the IT Services section, which is responsible for 'live' running and support. The handover normally occurs at the point when testing for live use can commence.

This module also covers the control and distribution of bought-in software (including operating system software, applications packages, PC software, etc) and documentation, where it exists in an electronic software format. It does not cover the control and distribution of hard-copy printed material.

2.4 Related guidance

This book is one of a series of modules issued as part of the CCTA IT Infrastructure Library. Although this module can be read in isolation, it should be used in conjunction with other IT Infrastructure Library modules. The following IT Infrastructure Library modules are relevant.

2.4.1 Configuration management

The **Configuration Management** module describes procedures for applying configuration management principles to organizations' IT infrastructures. SC&D is part of configuration management. SC&D deals with the physical control, distribution and implementation of software, under configuration management control. Configuration management is concerned with maintaining a logical model of the IT infrastructure, held in the CMDB, and of authorized changes to be made to it.

Whenever entirely new software, or new versions of existing software, are added to the DSL, details of the software must be simultaneously included in the CMDB. The CMDB contains up-to-date status information on all authorized software, and is used to ensure that all correct components, and only the correct components, are included in a software release.

2.4.2 Change management

The **Change Management** module describes procedures that ensure that all proposed changes are subjected to an authorization process, including assessment for impact and resource requirements. The Change Advisory Board (CAB) is the body that oversees the assessment. The CAB makes recommendations to IT management on whether to proceed with a change and makes proposals about which release the changes are to be scheduled into. The SC&D manager is responsible for implementing software releases in accordance with the requirements of IT management. The SC&D manager is normally a member of the CAB and is involved in establishing the organization's release policy.

2.4.3 Testing software for operational use

The module **Testing Software for Operational Use** describes procedures for the testing of software releases and other software items to be implemented on organizations' IT infrastructures. When software is accepted from the developers/suppliers it is placed in the DSL (and registered in the CMDB). The SC&D team is responsible for building releases from the DSL into the test environment(s). When testing is successfully concluded the SC&D team builds the live releases from the DSL and distributes them to the live environment(s).

2.4.4 Problem management and Help Desk

The **Problem Management** and **Help Desk** modules describe procedures for incident and problem control.

Problem management staff, Help Desk staff and other incident control staff must be informed about all new software releases, to help them to diagnose any incidents or problems that occur with the releases. Such staff must be trained in any new or revised procedures that apply as a result of implementing new software. Information on known errors affecting new software releases must be passed to them. Problem management staff are also often involved in identifying faults which will lead to requests for change (RFCs) and eventually result in new software releases.

2.5 Standards

ISO 9000 series, EN29000 and BS5750 - Quality Management and Quality Assurance Standards

The IT Infrastructure Library codes of practice are being designed to assist adherents to obtain third-party quality certification to ISO9001. Organizations' IT Directorates may wish to be so certified and CCTA will in future recommend that Facilities Management providers are also certified.

SSADM and PRINCE

SSADM is the recommended standard systems analysis and design method used in Government whilst PRINCE is the recommended standard project management method.

3. Planning software control and distribution

This section describes the activities involved in planning a SC&D function. It explains the need for a Definitive Software Library and describes how to plan release build, distribution and implementation procedures. The section also gives guidance on deciding a general policy for the change-content, size and frequency of software releases.

Like the rest of this module, this section applies to software developed in-house and bought-in. Special considerations regarding bought-in software are covered in section 3.1.10.

Figure 1(overleaf) shows the normal flow of software through various stages from its initial development/ purchase into the live environment.

The process begins with software being ordered or with software development being commissioned.

The software is then supplied and is subjected to quality control checks, to which the SC&D Manager is a party. These are described in section 3.1.5.5. If the delivered software does not satisfy the checks, rectification action is instigated (eg if sign-off by the Applications Development Manager has not been done, then either this should be done now or the software should be rejected).

If the quality control checks are successful the software is authorized for acceptance and copied into the DSL. For contingency purposes the DSL must be archived whenever its contents are altered and at regular intervals.

The content and timing of each release are decided and authorized in advance by change management. A release record is created and details are recorded in the CMDB. (The contents may, however, have to change as release development proceeds.) When all relevant software items are ready, the release is 'built' in the test environment. The test-build and test-running environments can be separate from each other. If that is the case, the release is copied into the test-running environment(s). 'Live-use' testing (operational-acceptance testing) is then carried out.

If testing shows that there is an unacceptable level of errors, rectification action is instigated. For example, if software changes are needed to rectify the errors, the software is referred back to the developer/supplier for eventual resubmission to the 'acceptance into the DSL' and subsequent 'testing' phases.

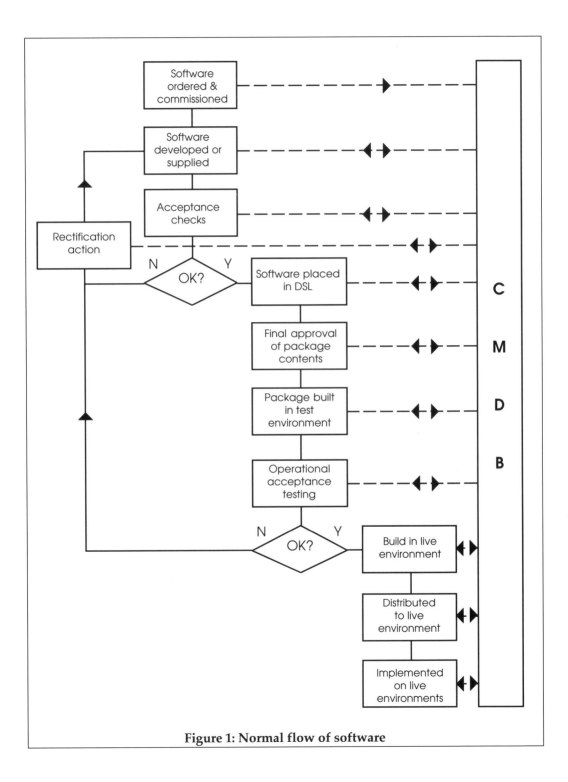

Figure 1: Normal flow of software

When live-use testing has been satisfactorily completed, authorization is given to release the software into the live environment(s). For software developed under the control of a PRINCE project, release authorization requires Operations Acceptance and User Acceptance letters.

The contents of the release are built in a live build environment according to the documentation held and correctly maintained up-to-date in the release record in the CMDB. The live-build and live-running environments can be the same, particularly if there is only one live-running environment. Once built, the release is distributed to each computer where it is required, and switched into live use.

Note that a complete build in the live environment is usually required, rather than simply copying over the release from the test environment. This is because there is no guarantee that the test environment is identical to the live environment and so the software as built in the test environment might not actually work in the live environment. Building in the live environment also ensures that the build process works in that environment and can be repeated if necessary.

It is important that the CMDB is kept constantly up to date. Activities arising from each of the stages shown in figure 1 must be immediately logged to the CMDB. Where possible this should be done automatically.

Each of these stages is described more fully in later sections of this module. It should be noted that several different releases can be at different stages of planning or activity concurrently.

Amended procedures apply for urgent releases. See section 3.1.4.5 for details.

3.1 Procedures

The IT Services Manager must appoint a Software Control & Distribution Manager, whose role will be to plan, implement and run the SC&D function. See Annex B for a suggested job description; see also section 3.3.3. It is strongly recommended that this post is combined with that of Configuration Manager.

Once appointed the SC&D Manager must carry out the following activities.

3.1.1 Agree overall objective

The overall objective for the SC&D function must be agreed with the IT Services Manager. It is recommended that this objective should read:

> "To contribute to the provision of quality IT services by ensuring that all software assets of the organization are securely controlled and that only correct versions of authorized software, appropriately tested, are in live use."

3.1.2 Staff recruitment and training

The SC&D Manager must decide the number and skill levels of SC&D staff required and instigate their recruitment.

The factors to be taken into account when considering staff numbers include:

* the number of software CIs to be controlled and the size, frequency and complexity of software changes/releases (eg number of items in a release, number of lines of code per item, etc) - generally speaking the larger, more frequent and more complex the changes/releases are, the greater the staff effort required

* the number of computers to which software releases have to be distributed and implemented - once again the larger the number the greater the likely effort

* the extent to which support tools are available - as far as possible, tools should be available to automate or assist in the SC&D processes, otherwise greater manual effort is required

* whether 'hardcopy' representations of software, for example program listings, are also to be stored and controlled (often no longer necessary, but there is sometimes reluctance to dispense with them) - if so further effort is required.

Further guidance on staff numbers and skill levels is given in section 3.3.4.

Training must be planned for all SC&D staff. This should include training in the principles and practices of configuration management and SC&D, as well as in use of appropriate support tools and software utilities.

3.1.3 Awareness campaign

Plan and execute an awareness campaign aimed at everyone who will be affected by the new SC&D function. This campaign may consist of holding seminars and distributing leaflets or circulars. The function's chances of success will increase if those using it have conviction that it provides the organization with real benefits, and has not just been arbitrarily decreed from above. Section 6 describes the benefits of SC&D.

Everyone should be told how they will be affected. At the outset only general information is likely to be available. As planning for the SC&D function proceeds, more details will emerge. Before the function goes live, everyone involved should have training in any new procedures that may affect them.

3.1.4 Plan release policy

The organization must plan and document its overall release policy, to provide a framework within which change management and SC&D are to work. The policy must be kept under review and amended if appropriate (see 5.1.5).

3.1.4.1 Release units

Start by stipulating the 'unit' levels at which software items should **normally** be released. The unit may vary depending on the type or item of software.

Figure 2 gives a simplified example showing an IT infrastructure made up of systems, which are in turn made up of suites, comprising programs which are made up of modules (for the purposes of this example hardware and network configuration items have been omitted).

The general aim is to decide the most appropriate release-unit level for each software item or type of software.

An organization could for example decide that the normal release unit for its Transaction Processing (TP) services should be at system level. Such a policy would mean that each time a CI forming part of the TP service was changed, a full release of the whole of that system would normally be issued.

The same organization may decide that a more appropriate release unit for a particular batch application should be the suite, whilst the release unit for another batch application should be at program level.

Figure 2:
Software
breakdown

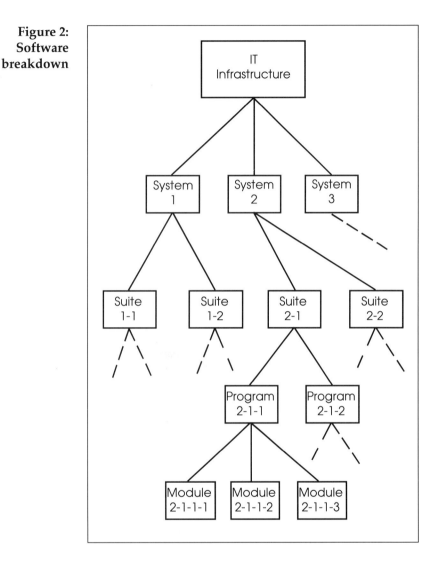

The following factors should be taken into account when deciding release units:

 * the amount of change necessary, overall and at each possible unit level (eg a high incidence of change affecting only particular modules within a program may allow the release unit to be one or more modules, whereas a high incidence of change affecting many modules at the same time may dictate that the release unit is the program, or something higher)

* the amount of resources and time needed to build, test, distribute and implement releases at each possible unit level - generally speaking, the larger the release unit the greater the SC&D and testing resources and effort that will be required to effect a given set of changes

* ease of implementation (eg if users are responsible for implementing new software on their own PCs, it is desirable to simplify this process as much as possible and to keep to a minimum the frequency with which it is needed: so, for example, it may be decided to issue a complete program instead of just amended modules)

* the complexity of interfaces between the proposed unit and the rest of the IT infrastructure (ie how easily this part can be 'detached' to form a relatively freestanding unit for building, testing and implementation).

It is particularly important to be aware that there is a limit to the number of changes that can satisfactorily be included in any release, and the size of the release should not exceed what can be comfortably built and tested. Equally, it is likely to be wasteful to have frequent releases with little change-content if less frequent releases with somewhat greater change-content can meet business requirements. The larger the amount of change implemented at any one time the greater is the risk of IT service problems, and the larger the release the greater the cost; but one larger release can often be less risky and cheaper than several smaller ones. See also 3.1.4.3 and 3.1.4.4.

When there is a choice about which changes to include in a release it is generally better to confine the changes to the lowest unit level that is practical. For example, several changes in one module are probably easier to test than one change in each of several modules, and clearly it is cheaper to build a module-level release than a program-level one.

Note that operational acceptance testing may have to be carried out at a different level from the unit of release. If, for example, a single software module is released, it may nevertheless be necessary to test the full program or suite. In general, however, testing is concentrated on units that are new or have been changed.

Note, too, that items that have not changed may be re-released to conform to release unit-level policy. Technically, such re-releasing is not strictly necessary if all software is under tight configuration management and SC&D control (see 3.1.4.2).

In extreme cases where the entire IT infrastructure is subject to frequent and wide-ranging changes, the organization may decide that the best policy is to allow the change manager, in collaboration with the SC&D manager, to decide the appropriate unit level by judging each case on its merits.

3.1.4.2 Delta releases

A delta release is one that includes only those CIs within the release unit that have actually changed or are new since the last full or delta release (eg if the release unit is the program a delta release contains only those modules that have changed, or are new, since the last full release of the program or the last delta release of the modules).

There may be occasions when release of a full unit is not justifiable. In such cases a delta release may be more appropriate. A decision must be made on whether delta releases will be allowed, and under what circumstances.

The major advantage of full releases is that all components of the release unit are built, tested, distributed and implemented together. There is no danger that obsolete versions of CIs that are wrongly thought to be unchanged will be used within the release. There is less temptation to short-circuit testing of supposedly unchanged CIs and of the interfaces from changed CIs to unchanged ones.

Any problems are therefore more likely to be detected and rectified before entry into the live environment. The disadvantage is that the amount of time, effort and computing resources needed to build, test, distribute and implement the release will increase. Although in some circumstances the testing of a delta release may need to be as extensive as that for an equivalent full release, the amount of building effort required to test a delta release is less than for a full release.

If the release is large and/or has to be distributed to a large number of installations, the additional effort associated with a full release can be considerable. For example, if the new release is needed only to effect a minor change - perhaps an emergency 'fix'- then a full release may be difficult to justify (for this reason urgent releases are more likely to be of the delta type; please see 3.1.4.5).

There is no single 'correct' choice. It is recommended that delta releases are allowed, with the decision being taken case-by-case. In each case the Change Advisory Board (CAB) must make a recommendation, based upon all the relevant facts, on whether the release unit stipulated in the release policy is appropriate or whether a delta release is preferable. In making its recommendation, the CAB must take into account:

* the size of a delta release in comparison with a full release, and hence the resources and effort required

* how urgently the facilities to be provided by the release are needed by the users

* the number of CIs (below the release unit level) that have changed since the last full release - a very large number may enforce a full release

* the possible impact upon the business if compatibility errors are found in the release (eg would it be preferable to wait for a full release than to risk interface problems arising with a delta release?)

* the resources available for building, testing, distributing and implementing the release (eg if implementation is to be via non-technical staff, would it be easier to implement a complete new release than a delta release?).

3.1.4.3 Package releases

To provide longer periods of stability for the live environment by reducing the frequency of releases, it is recommended that, where appropriate and where the resulting larger amount of change can be confidently handled without problems, individual releases (full units, delta releases or both) are grouped together to form 'package releases'. For example, changes to one system or suite will often require changes to be made to others. If all these changes have to be made at the same time, they should be included in the same package release.

A package could, for example, contain an initial version of a new TP service, several new versions of batch programs, and a number of new and initial versions of individual modules. Both full and delta releases can be included.

The use of package releases can reduce the likelihood of old or incompatible software being wrongly kept in use. It can encourage organizations to ensure that all changes that should be made concurrently, in different suites and systems, are actually made concurrently, and to test the interworking of these suites and systems fully.

Care should be taken, however, not to exceed, in any particular package release, the amount of change that can comfortably be handled.

3.1.4.4 Frequency and change-content of releases

The proposed maximum and typical release frequencies, and the amount of change-content in each release, should be agreed for all types of software and of releases. These planned frequencies and change-content limits will provide overall guidance; particular releases will have to be scheduled by change management in the light of circumstances and it may not be possible in all circumstances to adhere to the planned frequencies and change-content limits.

In general the changes to be applied to IT infrastructures are governed by business needs, user requirements and technical considerations. There is a need to allow for releases frequent enough to accommodate all necessary changes without exceeding the sizes of releases and the amount of change-content in them that can be comfortably accommodated. However, releases that are too frequent may result in higher costs and a lack of stability compared with the use of larger less frequent releases. A balance must be made between the need to incorporate new facilities and/or correct problems with previous versions as soon as possible, and the costs and lack of stability that may be caused by too frequent releases. Although the IT infrastructure may become more stable overall if the frequency of releases is reduced by means of larger releases, the risk of errors affecting any one release is greater. Care should be taken to reduce such risks, by ensuring adherence to all change management, configuration management, testing and SC&D procedures. At times of particular business dependency on IT, software changes should be avoided if possible.

When a change to some CIs requires that other CIs are changed at the same time, it may be impossible to avoid making some releases bigger than ideally they ought to be.

Planning guidelines for the frequency and change-content of releases must take into account the organization's planned release-unit levels and its policy on delta releases and package releases. It is best to make decisions on all these items at the same time.

3.1.4.5 Urgent releases

Despite careful planning and testing, there will be occasions when urgent fixes are necessary to resolve very severe or high priority problems. In such cases a request for a special urgent release is submitted to the change management system and evaluated by the Change Advisory Board Executive Committee (CAB/EC). Based on the recommendations of the CAB/EC, the Change Manager decides whether to authorize an urgent release. If it is authorized, the urgent release is inserted in between, and in addition to, normal releases. In the majority of cases the urgency of the requirement means that a delta release will be used.

Procedures for handling urgent releases must ensure that great care is taken. Despite the urgency, a number of important safeguards must still be maintained:

* the definitive version of the software, stored in and obtained from the DSL, must always be used as a basis for the emergency release, and changed to effect the fix - this ensures the correct software is used

* for software developed in-house, the source code must be changed to effect the fix, and a copy of the amended source code must be stored in the DSL to be used as the basis for any future changes that have to be made

* all urgent releases must be subjected to, and approved by, change management (please see the **Change Management** module for details of urgent change procedures)

* all actions must be done under configuration management control and must be reflected in the CMDB (this of course applies to all releases, but is easier to overlook in an emergency)

* the version number of the software must be incremented to reflect the changes that have been made

* whatever testing is possible within the time available should be carried out

* as much notice as possible should be given to the users about the release (this would normally be done via the Help Desk)

* any necessary documentation changes (eg an amendment to a user guide) must be carried out as soon as possible - change management and SC&D procedures should set target times by which new permanent documentation must be issued, but if temporary documentation or instructions are needed these should be produced and issued to coincide with the urgent release.

The incidence of urgent releases must be kept to a minimum - they disrupt the normal planned release cycle, and are error prone.

3.1.4.6 Release numbering

Each release must be allocated a release number. A 2 or 3 level number is recommended with the top level being reserved for major releases and the bottom level for minor releases.

It is normal to allocate each release a version number for use during the building and testing processes. If unacceptable errors are identified during testing, changes must be made to the contents of the release, and the version number must be incremented accordingly.

For further details on version numbering please see the **Configuration Management** module.

3.1.5 Plan the Definitive Software Library (DSL)

Plans must be made for the DSL. This library is a secure compound (a logical storage area) in which the definitive authorized versions of all software CIs are stored and protected. This one logical storage area may in reality consist of one or more software libraries or file storage areas which must be separate from development, test or live filestore areas.

A physical floppy disc store for definitive copies of PC software should also exist and will form part of the logical DSL. Please see section 3.1.10.2 for further details.

3.1.5.1 Hardware/ operating system environment

The DSL filestore need not be part of the same hardware/ operating system environment on which the releases built from the DSL will run. In fact there are strong security arguments for consolidating the entire IT Directorate's DSL into a separate environment (eg on a separate machine from the live environment - though this may be difficult to cost justify in small installations with only one machine - or stored on dedicated disc volumes which are not normally in use). The link between the DSL and the rest of the IT infrastructure can then be severed, except for those times when access is needed to add new software or to extract software during release building.

In some large multi-node IT infrastructures it may even prove possible to dispense completely with the need for compilers and source code in the live-running environments, thus significantly improving security. Releases are built in a live-build environment and distributed to the live-running environments and switched into use.

Some configuration management support tools incorporate software libraries, which can be regarded as a logical part of a DSL.

3.1.5.2 Storage of code

For software developed in-house, code is normally stored in the DSL as source rather than object. The build process consists of compiling and collecting/link editing the source code in order to produce object code for running on the run-time environments. Bought-in software is, however, normally supplied in object form only and so will have to be stored as such. Documents are normally held in the DSL as text files rather than print files, to save a small amount of space and to make them more universally accessible (eg more easily transferred into alternative software packages such as different word processing or desk-top publishing systems).

3.1.5.3 Sizing the DSL

The SC&D Manager must, in conjunction with the Capacity Manager, estimate the space needed at the outset to accommodate the DSL. Where existing software is to be taken under formal control, the actual storage requirements will already be known (though may have to be 'converted' if the DSL storage medium is different from that currently being used). Where the DSL is to contain 'new' software, which is not yet in existence, estimates of individual file sizes must be obtained from the system designers.

Another important factor to be taken into account is the number of generations of software that are to be retained in the DSL. It is recommended that a minimum of two previous versions, plus the current version, of all software

are retained in the DSL. Where filestore limitations prevent this, previous versions must be archived using magnetic tapes or some other appropriate form of media, but it should be recognized that this may cause delays should reversion to a previous version be necessary.

When sizing the DSL, note that space should be allowed for all software required for current and archived build and run-time environments, both test and live.

It is also necessary to take into account future space requirements. Account should be taken of proposals for entirely new software, and new versions of existing software. Previous records may be a source of information from which future trends may be extrapolated, but proposed business plans or likely legislative changes should also be examined to determine their probable impact.

When the sizing is complete, the SC&D Manager must negotiate with the Capacity Manager to obtain the necessary filestore, both for the DSL and for archive media. If new media or hardware is needed, procurement must be instigated.

3.1.5.4 Security of the DSL

It is essential that source code in the DSL is kept up to date and free from corruption. Otherwise the live system becomes unmaintainable.

In the event of disaster or corruption affecting part or all of the live or test IT systems, the normal course of action should be to revert to regularly taken back-up copies of the live or test object code respectively. If this is not possible or proves unsuccessful (eg there is a software virus that has also affected the back-ups), it is vital that the system can be reconstituted from the authorized, configuration managed, source code, system software and other software in the DSL.

It is therefore very important that strict controls restrict access to the DSL to SC&D personnel only.

Procedures for regular back-up of the contents of the DSL, with remote storage to cater for disaster situations, must also be planned and documented.

3.1.5.5 Adding software to the DSL

The rules under which software may be added to the DSL must be clearly defined. This will safeguard the contents of the DSL and minimize the prospect of unauthorized software entering the DSL. These rules must include checks that:

* all items are *bona fide*, and have genuinely been ordered or commissioned - this will require documented procedures for SC&D staff which specifically identify from whom each software item or class of software can be accepted

* all software is as expected and no malicious additions are included (this is a particular problem with PC software packages - see section 3.1.10.2 for further details)

* all developed software has successfully passed a quality review, which has been documented and which has been signed-off by the post-holder responsible

* new versions of software have been developed from the correct, definitive previous version - and not, for instance, based on development copies that may have been in existence

* only correct, definitive utility and system software is used to create new software for inclusion in the DSL

* all amendments to previous versions have been authorized by change management and no other amendments have been included - this may require file comparison facilities (eg ICL's Match_Records)

* all items to be added to the DSL have been correctly logged in the CMDB; the CMDB must be updated when the items are added (if this does not happen automatically as part of the file transfer into the DSL)

* all relevant licence fees have been correctly paid, and all irrelevant ones stopped.

3.1.5.6 Releasing software for testing and live use

Operational acceptance testing of software is carried out on the releases that it is proposed will eventually go into the live environments. Each test release is built from the DSL. SC&D must not accept a release for building onto the live environments until it has been successfully tested and signed-off by the testing manager. There must be full documentation on the number and severity of known errors - see the IT Infrastructure Library **Problem Management** module.

When successful testing is concluded, the test release is not normally copied directly into the live environments. Instead the live release is re-built from the DSL and implemented in the live environments. This is done because there is no guarantee that a software release working in a test environment will necessarily work in the live environments. This process also ensures that only definitive software is used for the build and that the build process actually works in the live build environment and can be repeated, should it be necessary. When the live release is working satisfactorily the test release is deleted from the test environment.

Further details on operational acceptance testing are contained in the IT Infrastructure Library module **Testing Software for Operational Use**.

3.1.6 Plan procedures for building software releases

Procedures must be planned and documented for building software releases.

The Change Manager, acting on recommendations from the Change Advisory Board (CAB), is responsible for scheduling the content and timing of releases. The SC&D Manager must be a member of the CAB and participate in the scheduling of software releases. Details of change management procedures can be found in the **Change Management** module.

A forward schedule of proposed releases should be decided by the Change Manager and published in advance to all interested parties.

When a new release is scheduled, configuration management creates a 'release record' in the CMDB. The release record is itself a CI which must be controlled accordingly. The release record itemizes all the CIs that will be included in that release and is used later during the release build to ensure that the contents are as intended and authorized.

If the Change Manager amends the contents of a release, perhaps due to failures encountered during testing or changed business priorities, then the release record must be amended accordingly.

Figure 3 shows a typical example of the sequencing of releases.

Figure 3:
Example release
sequence

STAGE / DATE	TEST	LIVE	ARCHIVE
1.1.91	V1.0		
1.4.91	V2.0	V1.0	
9.5.91	V1.1 V2.0	V1.0	
16.5.91	V2.0	V1.1	V1.0
1.7.91	V3.0	V2.0	V1.1 V1.0
1.10.91		V3.0	V2.0 1.1 1.0
1.12.91	V4.0	V3.0	V2.0 1.1 1.0

In this example, which assumes a single operational acceptance testing stage, the sequencing of events is as follows:

1 Jan 91 - Version 1.0 is built and implemented in the test environment.

1 Apr 91 - Version 1.0 has been successfully tested and is now re-built and implemented in the live environment; version 2.0 is ready for testing and is built and implemented in the test environment.

9 May 91 - Version 1.0 is still in live use but an important small amendment has been proposed. It is not possible to wait for the next scheduled full release so a delta release (described in section 3.1.4.2), version 1.1, has been scheduled and is built and implemented for testing. The testing of version 2 continues in parallel, but it now also embodies the amendment that was incorporated in version 1.1.

16 May 91 - Version 1.1 has been successfully tested and is therefore rebuilt and implemented in the live environment. Version 1.0 is archived away and retained in case reversion is required. Version 2.0 is still undergoing testing.

1 Jul 91 - Version 2.0 has been successfully tested and is re-built and implemented in the live environment. Version 1.1 is archived and retained. The next scheduled release (version 3.0) is ready for testing and so is built and implemented in the test environment.

1 Oct 91 - Version 3.0 has been successfully tested and implemented in the live environment. Version 2.0 is archived and retained along with versions 1.0 and 1.1.

1 Dec 91 - Version 4.0 commences testing.

The process of building software releases normally includes the following activities:

* accessing the CMDB for the relevant release record

* identifying from the release record current versions of the software CIs to be included in the release, and confirming that all required versions are available in the DSL (or will be by the time they are needed)

* marshalling these CIs from the DSL into the build environment (see below)

* conducting the actual build (compiling, link-editing, etc - see below)

* creating and documenting a record of the build process (this should be a chronological record of all the processes carried out and should include all job journals for compilations, etc).

Conducting the actual build involves, as a minimum, compiling and linking application modules produced in-house and any bought-in software that is held in source form, in each case from the DSL. It may also involve incorporation into the release of any bought-in software, in object form, that is to be included. It may include generating databases and populating them with test data or, for live builds, static reference data (eg the Post Office Address File). Where necessary, it includes generation (or, minimally, transcription from the DSL) of the operating system, the DBMS run-time components, etc.

All job control software, parameters, test data, run-time software and any other software that is required for the release must be under configuration management control and must have been subject to quality control checks before being stored in the DSL. At build time the required software items that do not already exist in the build or run-time environment should be copied, along with the applications code, from the DSL to the build environment for release building. A complete record of the build process must be logged in the CMDB.

This arrangement facilitates total repeatability of the build, should it be necessary.

**Figure 4:
DSL on Test
or Live node**

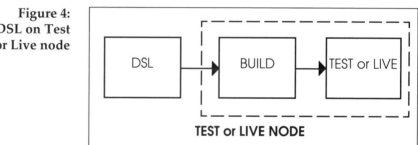

Software releases can often be built directly into the test or live environments (either on the same computer node as the DSL as shown in figure 4 or on a separate node as shown in figure 5, overleaf). In this arrangement the live node is likely to be the same node as the test one.

Building a release directly into a test or live environment may however be impractical, particularly if software releases are to be built centrally for distribution to a number of remote locations, or if security considerations dictate that there should be no compilers, link editors, etc, on the live/test environments. In such cases, a separate test- or live-build environment is needed. The build environments are

Figure 5:
DSL not on Test
or Live node

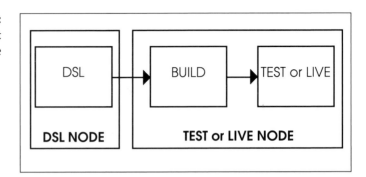

the environments used to build test and live releases. They exactly mirror the test and live run-time environments, except that the run-time environments may not have compilers, etc, present.

The built software is stored in the build environment ready for distribution (see figure 6). If one or more build environments are necessary, they should be planned and sized in a similar way to the DSL. More than one build environment may be needed if, for example, software with the same functionality needs distributing to 200 type A distributed PCs and to 30 type B small mainframes. Two test build and two live build environments would therefore be necessary with the different characteristics of the two target machine types (A and B).

Figure 6:
Use of a build
environment

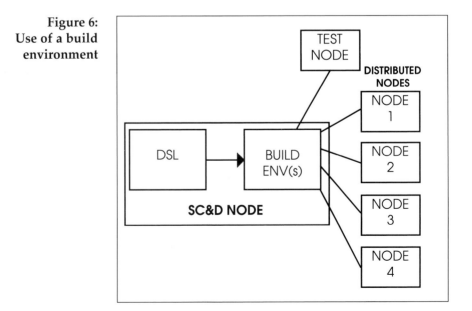

3.1.7 Plan software distribution and implementation procedures

Procedures must be planned for distributing software releases from the test build environment into the test environment, and from the live build environment into the live environment(s), and for bringing them into use - implementing them - in these environments.

Where the build environment is not resident on the same computer as the appropriate test or live environment(s), it is necessary to use a communications link or some form of portable magnetic medium (removable disk or tape).

All reasonable steps must be taken to obviate the possibility of software corruption during distribution to the target environment. Any technical aids available (eg checksums on the data transmission), should be used to detect errors so that corrective action can be taken.

As well as transmitting the content of the build to a target environment, it is often necessary to execute some additional processes on the target machine to enable operation of the new software to commence. This may involve such actions as archiving of superseded software versions and loading of existing live data into a new database structure; and will almost always involve some 'switch on' action such as a library switch.

If the same software release is to be distributed for use at a large number of locations, it may be essential for all users to start using the new release at the same time (eg if a mandatory legal change is to be introduced nationwide at start of business on a specific day, or if a distributed corporate database is involved). If the release is to be implemented in many locations concurrently, special steps may be necessary. Scale may determine that distribution of the release to all locations has to be spread over a period of time, but the dormant release can be installed at each location in readiness for live implementation, with some form of 'switch' triggered to bring all releases into use at the appropriate time. The switch may involve issuing of a command from a terminal at either a central control site or at a number of distributed sites. Alternatively, some form of software switch may be embedded in the release itself, to be activated upon some predefined event.

All necessary job control software and parameters for use at implementation-time must be controlled in essentially the same way as those for build-time (see section 3.1.6). The objective is to make the implementation process as simple, foolproof and secure as possible. Ideally the SC&D team should only need to issue a single command from a terminal or console to execute the implementation process, once transmission of the release has been successfully completed. It should also be possible to check from the distribution centre that the implementation has been successful. If transmission is via magnetic media then some 'local' actions are unavoidable, though ideally this should be limited to physically mounting the tapes or disks, updating local procedures and manuals, etc.

Unless the distribution and implementation process can be controlled automatically, or from the centre using software tools, human procedures must ensure that distributed software arrives when expected and is checked in whatever way is practical for authenticity; and that the software is brought into use when required. These procedures must include the following activities:

* central SC&D staff to inform remote staff when to expect distributed software to arrive

* remote staff report to the central SC&D staff when the distributed software has arrived successfully

* central SC&D staff to check that all software is received as expected at remote locations

* central SC&D staff to issue clear instructions about **when** the software is to be implemented

* remote staff to report to the centre when the software **has been** implemented.

The release record on the CMDB states which installations are to receive the release. The CMDB must be updated to reflect the receipt and implementation of the release at each remote site.

Change management procedures require that back-out plans are made in advance for all changes that are to be implemented. In the case of new software releases this will normally involve withdrawal of the new release and reversion to the previous trusted release. This may not however be possible (eg the new release implements a mandatory legislative change - so it is obviously not possible to use the old program versions). In such cases alternative back-out plans must be made. In all cases the back-out plans must, where possible, be tested and proved to be workable.

3.1.8 Rework

Whenever it is necessary (eg as a result of a Request for Change (RFC)) to carry out any rework on software that is under formal SC&D control, the definitive source code version held in the DSL must be used as a basis for the re-work. Once the re-working is complete, and re-worked versions of the software have passed quality control checks, this new version must be placed in the DSL.

Applications developers must not be allowed to base re-working on versions of software that may exist within their own libraries, as these may be subtly different from the authorized quality-controlled versions in the DSL. The cooperation of the application developers is needed to ensure this rule is obeyed. If necessary their working procedures must be amended. Checks must be made by applications development managers to ensure that these procedures are complied with.

3.1.9 Hard copy storage

The organization must decide whether the precaution of keeping hard copies of source listings, etc, is warranted. These may be useful for reference at times when the relevant computers are unavailable, or for comparison or reference by the computer auditors.

If hard copies are to be held, physical storage space is needed to accommodate them. For large systems a significant amount of space may be needed. Hard copies are often held to serve as diagnostic aids following a disaster. If this is a requirement, steps must be taken to safeguard them, probably off-site. For further information please refer to the IT Infrastructure Library **Contingency Planning** module.

3.1.10 Procedures for bought-in software

The following additional procedures are necessary for bought-in software.

3.1.10.1 Bought-in Mainframe/Mini software

In general the procedures to be planned for managing bought-in software for use on mainframes/minis are the same as those for software developed in-house, though with the following exceptions.

It is likely that non-modifiable object (rather than source) code will be supplied. This will not be subject to modification/re-work, other than exceptionally under suppliers' instructions. It is still necessary, however, to lodge a copy of the object code in the DSL and to effect movement into and out of the DSL under configuration management control.

Items of bought-in software must from time-to-time be built into the build, test and live environments. New or modified bought-in software items should be included in a release with other software if the bought-in software and the other software must be introduced into the environments at the same time. If the new or changed bought-in software is needed to support the other software, the bought-in software can be introduced in the live environment before the other software, if that is feasible and more convenient. Any required modifications to bought-in software should be made from the copy in the DSL.

3.1.10.2 Bought-in PC software packages

As PC software packages are likely to be delivered on floppy discs, and licences may prohibit copying (unless a multiple licence is held), it is absolutely essential that the original floppy discs are stored and controlled. A physical floppy disc store should therefore be created. This store can be regarded as part of the logical DSL.

Prior to entry into the store the software must be checked to ensure that it is as expected and that it contains no malicious additions. The CCTA IT Security Library **Viruses and Other Malicious Software** document outlines the steps that should be carried out.

Any authorized copies of PC packages that are made by the SC&D team must be allocated a unique copy number and recorded in the CMDB together with details of where they are located and who is responsible for them. All changes that occur must be recorded in the CMDB (eg a change of location, a fault which is detected). Procedural restrictions should be introduced to prohibit the unauthorized copying of PC software, and regular software audits should include a check for any unauthorized copies.

The most common entry path of software viruses is via pirate copies of games software or utility software brought into an organization without authorization. Organizations' procedures should expressly prohibit the loading of such software on any PC. Disciplinary action should be taken against offenders who breach these procedures. Consideration should be given to making available to users only PCs that do not include floppy disc drives, unless these are required for other purposes, as this will guarantee that software cannot be copied from or to floppy discs using such PCs.

The installation and implementation of package software onto individual PCs may involve little or no effort (eg all that may be required could be to insert a floppy disc in a drive and press a command key). However, for networks involving large numbers of PCs, considerable effort may be needed to distribute and install the software (eg 1000 copies may have to be distributed, installed and implemented nationwide). Depending upon licensing conditions and networking capabilities it may be possible to download the 1000 copies to the PCs, rather than physically distributing 1000 floppy discs.

If central distribution via a network is impossible, and the software is free standing, an alternative is to allow the users to install and implement the software for themselves, but there are dangers in this. Some users may not implement the package when they are supposed to and some may try and fail. This may result in different versions on different PCs at the same time, which could be unacceptable.

One way of alleviating these problems is to have the users copy their newly implemented software to floppy disc and then to return the disc to the SC&D team for checking that the implementation has been carried out correctly.

In general however, where practicable, it is safer to leave software implementation to SC&D staff. It can be controlled better, which should result in higher quality IT service.

The terms and conditions relating to the purchase of PC software may place legal restrictions on the organization (eg no unauthorized copies to be made). It is particularly important therefore, regardless of who carries out the implementation, that the CMDB is updated with details of who holds copies of software items. This assists the organization to discharge its legal obligations, and assists auditors, and the help desk, to check for the existence of unauthorized copies.

Further information about the control of PCs can be found in the **Management of Local Processors and Terminals** module.

3.1.11 Internally created PC software

It is important that internally created PC software, including document files, should be controlled and managed in a similar manner to other software.

Version numbers must be used and incremented whenever changes are made. Unless it is absolutely clear that a proposed change will not impact on parts of the organization other than the author, the proposal must be submitted for authorization to change management.

A new file should be created each time a new version is required, rather than overwriting the previous version; this approach leaves a regression path and gives an historical record of the previous versions. If an item of PC software is undergoing heavy development or enhancement, a new version should be 'baselined' at specific procedural points in time or at predefined steps in the development process. Such new versions should be lodged in the DSL where they will be protected, and available if required in the future. The CMDB must be updated with details of the addition to the DSL.

3.1.12 Identify support tool requirements

The SC&D Manager must identify the extent to which the various operating systems in use at central and remote locations provide facilities to assist in controlling and distributing software, and decide what additional support tools will be required. Section 7 lists the required facilities and gives examples of tools available at the time of writing (1990). Note that tools for SC&D are often marketed as configuration management support tools - see also the IT Infrastructure Library **Configuration Management** module.

When these requirements have been identified, procurement of the tools must be instigated.

3.1.13 Amendments to existing procedures

The SC&D Manager must work closely with other IT managers, including the Application Development Managers, the Computer Operations Manager, the Network Manager, the Change Manager, the Configuration Manager and the person in charge of operational acceptance testing, to ensure that their existing procedures are amended to interface with and complement the new SC&D procedures.

3.1.14 Documentation of SC&D procedures

Procedures for building, distribution and installation/ implementation of software releases, including the organization's software release policy, for the control and maintenance of the DSL, and for the management and use of any supporting tools and facilities, must be documented. This documentation must be reviewed by representatives of the IT staff affected by SC&D, then approved by the SC&D Manager and authorized by the IT Services Manager for issue. Amendments required to documentation to reflect changes in procedures or policy should be subject to normal change management control and properly authorized. Superseded versions of documentation should be withdrawn from use.

3.1.15 Devise implementation plan

Plans must be made for implementing the new SC&D system.

There are distinct advantages in limiting the initial coverage of the SC&D function to deliverables from new projects, in that:

* material initially builds up in the DSL relatively slowly, allowing familiarization with the procedures and support tools to be gained gradually

* the ethos of a new project may be such that team members are better disposed towards new SC&D procedures than software maintenance personnel who are used to previous procedures and may resist change

* initial 'release' activity will occur when the software from the new project is moved into the test environment and then, later, into the live environment. As this will be the initial version of new software, users will not yet have become dependent upon it, so any teething troubles with the new procedures will have less impact.

Consideration should therefore be given to planning the SC&D function to be ready to coincide with the delivery dates for one or more new projects.

For further guidance on what the implementation plan should include, please see section 4.1.

3.1.16 Plan the ongoing management and operation of SC&D

Plans must be made for the ongoing management and operation of the SC&D system. Section 5.1 covers the procedures that must be planned.

3.2 Dependencies

Commitment from senior IT management is required to initiate SC&D planning, and to win the support of the personnel who will have to interface with SC&D.

To be effective, SC&D is heavily dependent upon configuration management, change management and operational acceptance testing. If these functions do not already exist they must be planned in conjunction with the SC&D system.

3.3 People

The key people involved during the planning stages are:

* the Director of IT
* the IT Services Manager
* the SC&D Manager
* SC&D staff.

3.3.1 The Director of IT

The SC&D function is one of the responsibilities of the IT Services Manager (see 3.3.2). However, SC&D also affects staff, including applications development personnel, outside IT Services. For that reason in particular, the Director of IT must be seen to be committed to the new procedures and to assume overall responsibility for the successful implementation and running of SC&D.

3.3.2 The IT Services Manager

Under the Director of IT, the IT Services Manager is the head of the IT Services section, with overall responsibility for service quality. Typically his/her peer managers are the Applications Development Manager(s) and the Finance & Administration Manager (see figure 7). The SC&D Manager reports to the IT Services Manager.

**Figure 7:
Management
structure**

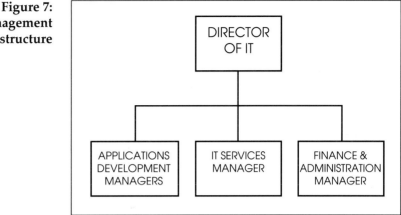

The IT Services Manager must initiate the whole process of installing a SC&D function, and take responsibility for winning the hearts and minds of personnel who will have to interface with SC&D.

3.3.3 The SC&D Manager

The SC&D Manager is appointed by, and reports to, the IT Services Manager and is responsible for the detailed planning and enabling activities prior to implementation of the SC&D function. It is strongly recommended that this post is combined with that of the Configuration Manager. Where possible it is also recommended that the role of Change Manager should be combined in this post.

The holder of the SC&D post must contribute significantly towards the overall goal of providing high quality IT services, so careful selection and good training are very important. A sound technical background, with a good understanding (or an ability to get it) of the IT infrastructure which is to be managed, and the services it provides; a good working knowledge of all support tools and utilities; and a good grasp of the principles and practices of IT infrastructure management - especially change management and configuration management - and of software maintenance and development, are essential. An awareness of the organization's business strategy and priorities is also needed. Staff management skills are highly desirable.

To help the SC&D Manager to attain these skills and to keep them up to date, full technical training must be given. Regular updates are required as technology changes.

Regular briefings on the organization's business position should also be given.

There is, as yet, no entry in the British Computer Society 'Industry Structure Model' (BCS/ISM) for this type of post, but it is recommended that the entry level experience, skill level and academic background should be broadly equivalent to either Senior Operations Manager (cell ref OP M 8) or Senior Systems Programmer (cell ref OP P 5). For Government organizations, normal Civil Service grading rules apply.

Supporting staff will be required in other than small installations.

3.3.4 SC&D staff

The number of SC&D staff needed depends on the scale of operations.

Because SC&D is on the critical path between applications development and live operations, and is involved in all important changes to live software, there should be enough trained staff to cover for annual leave and absences. The minimum practical staffing level is therefore at least two people - including the SC&D Manager - though where appropriate, such as in very small installations, one of these two could work part-time on SC&D and the other could be a 'reserve'.

At the opposite end of the scale, the Inland Revenue, Telford has a team of 4-5 people carrying out their IT infrastructure configuration management and SC&D activities, out of a total IT workforce of 1200.

Another example is the DSS/DE NUBS system, which has 6 staff, out of a total of approximately 300, employed on configuration management and SC&D activities (covering both IT infrastructure management and applications development projects).

SC&D staff should be given technical training in the principles and practices of change and configuration management and of software maintenance and development, and in the use of support tools and utilities. A more general awareness of the IT infrastructure and the services it provides should be imparted, together with an appreciation of the organization's business issues. This training should be regularly 'topped-up' as required. A record of all SC&D staff training should be documented and maintained.

Ideally all support staff should have an entry level experience, skill level and academic background equivalent to BCS/ISM Operator 3 (cell ref OP O 2) or Programmer 2 (cell ref OP P 2). If, however, it is necessary to take on trainee SC&D staff their academic background and experience and entry skill level should equate to Operator 2 (OP O 1) or Programmer 1 (OP P 1). For Government organizations, normal Civil Service grading rules apply.

3.3.5 Interfaces

The Applications Development, Operational Acceptance Test, Computer Operations and Network Managers, as well as the Configuration and Change Managers if these activities are separate from SC&D, are responsible for interfacing their own procedures to those of SC&D and for familiarizing and training their staff and themselves in the new procedures.

3.4 Timing

If configuration management and change management are in place, plan for SC&D immediately, with a view to implementing it as soon as possible. It is likely to take only a few weeks from the start of the planning stage to initial implementation, although this time may be extended by lead times for staff placement (re-deployment from other duties or recruitment) and any necessary procurement of hardware and support tools. Such lead times should be established and included when planning the timetable.

There are distinct advantages in limiting the initial coverage of the SC&D function to deliverables from new projects. Consideration should therefore be given to planning the implementation of the new SC&D function to coincide with the delivery dates for one or more new projects.

4. Implementation

4.1 Procedures

When the necessary staff, hardware and support tools are in place and all necessary training has been completed, the DSL and build environment(s) must be physically created and the necessary security permissions established to limit access to authorized SC&D staff. The DSL and build environments should be tested in accordance with criteria defined at the planning stage.

All staff affected by the changeover to the new SC&D arrangements must be informed about the implementation timetable. It must be made clear to them how they will be affected.

In particular, applications development staff must be told when to start delivering material to SC&D for inclusion in the DSL, and arrangements must be made for all bought-in software to be delivered directly to the SC&D team, for lodging in the DSL.

A gradual approach to implementation is recommended where possible (as indicated in 3.1.15). This can be achieved by initially taking under control only deliverables from new projects or newly bought-in software. When experience with the new procedures and tools has been gained and teething problems overcome, consideration can be given to bringing existing software under the control of the new SC&D procedures (see below). Such software must nevertheless be brought under configuration management control as soon as is practical, consistent with the effective and efficient provision of IT services.

Implementation of release control (building, distribution, and implementation) obviously occurs sometime after creation of the DSL. The release control procedures must be tested before they are brought into use. If a gradual approach has been adopted, as recommended, the first release build will be when the deliverables from the selected development project or from the chosen supplier, are to be subject to operational acceptance testing. By the time releases to the live environment are needed, the build and release control procedures will have been used for putting software into the operational acceptance testing environment, thereby providing another chance for many classes of potential problems with procedures and tools to be found and corrected.

Plans should, however, be made in case the new procedures or tools fail. If software releases are urgently required, it may be necessary to revert temporarily to previous procedures until the new procedures are corrected. Where possible, it is recommended that the procedures or tools for distributing software to remote sites are tested separately from those for implementing the software at the remote sites, thereby allowing problems with each of these phases to be isolated and corrected separately.

Although the procedures for the distribution of software to, and implementation of software on, remote sites should be thoroughly tested before being brought into live use, time should nevertheless be allowed to resolve any teething problems in the early stages of live use. It is no good, for example, bringing the distribution/implementation procedures into use the day before a vital item of software must be brought into use at 1000 sites nationwide!

If there has been a gradual approach to implementation, the take-on of software should proceed as follows. When existing software is replaced by different software, the replacements should be brought immediately under SC&D control. When existing software is subject to revision or enhancement, the replaced or enhanced items should be placed in the DSL, and the new release should be built from them under SC&D control. Eventually, when resources permit and the effort is judged cost effective, remaining software can be lodged in the DSL, subject to normal quality control checks, ready for any future rework. This work will be based on the SC&D release control procedures described in this module.

4.2 Dependencies

As stated earlier, SC&D is heavily dependent upon configuration management, change management and operational acceptance testing. If these functions do not already exist, then they must be implemented and must be operating successfully by the time the new SC&D function becomes operational.

Staff must have been trained in the new SC&D procedures, in the principles and practices of change and configuration management, and in the use of the hardware and software tools.

The DSL, build and run-time environments must have been created and tested, and support tools must have been procured, tested and installed before the SC&D function is brought into live use (note that support tools must themselves be configuration-managed).

Testing of the procedures and tools should be carried out by simulating live use, with trial software. As far as possible these trials should mirror the live processes and should test all aspects of the new SC&D system.

4.3 People

4.3.1 The SC&D Manager

The SC&D Manager is responsible for implementing and then running the new SC&D procedures, including notifying all those who interface with the SC&D function of the implementation date/time, and ensuring that they are familiar with the new procedures.

4.3.2 The Change Manager and CAB

The CAB is responsible for recommending that the new SC&D procedures are to be applied to a defined set of CIs that constitute a software release, and for recommending approval of the changes to be made to existing procedures to interface them to the new SC&D procedures. The Change Manager decides whether to accept the CAB recommendations.

The SC&D Manager is a member of the CAB and expresses his/her views on the proposed contents of releases and advises on SC&D section workload, etc, for scheduling purposes. Further details of the responsibilities and make-up of the CAB can be found in the IT Infrastructure Library **Change Management** module.

4.3.3 Interfaces

Upon full implementation of the new SC&D system, no software should be allowed on to the IT infrastructure via any other route and no software should be released for testing or live use, or for rework, except from the DSL via the new release control procedures. Interim arrangements may be needed for existing software that is not yet under SC&D control, but such software must nevertheless be placed as soon as possible under configuration management control and must not be amended in any way without authorization from change management.

Procedures for the hand-over of software from development projects, or the delivery of software from suppliers, should be amended to ensure this software is delivered to the DSL (once past quality control) and is installed by SC&D. Procedures for the maintenance and enhancement of software should be amended to ensure that software for rework is taken from the DSL, under SC&D control and that, once re-worked and past quality control, it is put into the DSL under SC&D control.

4.4 Timing

Implementation of the new procedures for acceptance of software should, if possible, be synchronized with the delivery of software from one or more development projects, or the delivery of purchased software from a supplier.

The new release control procedures should be available, tested as fully as possible, for the start of the operational acceptance testing of the selected software.

Time should be allowed to deal with any teething problems associated with the distribution and implementation of software, particularly for networked distributed systems. Initially several weeks contingency should be allowed but, as confidence in the new system improves, this interval can be reduced to perhaps only a few days. This time interval does not allow for the need to 'recover' from software that is of insufficient quality to 'go live'.

SC&D procedures should not be applied to existing software until the procedures have been thoroughly proven on new material. In the case of large systems, the effort in retrofitting the new procedures to old software will be far from trivial. If the potential problems appear to outweigh the advantages the retrofit should not be attempted. As software is replaced by new versions, over a period of time the new procedures can be gradually applied to all software, as described in 4.1. When the amount of software that is not under SC&D control is small - typically 20% to 5% of the total - consideration should be given to retrofitting SC&D to these remaining items, if it is cost-effective.

5. Post-implementation and audit

5.1 Procedures

This section covers the ongoing management and operations of SC&D. These processes have already been outlined in section 3.1, where they are also shown diagrammatically in figure 1.

5.1.1 Control of DSL

The SC&D team is responsible for the management and control of the DSL. The team must ensure that only authorized software is accepted into the DSL, that this software is protected whilst resident in the DSL, and that software is only copied from the DSL by authorized SC&D staff.

Close liaison is necessary with the configuration management team to ensure that changes to the contents of the DSL are made under configuration management control, and are recorded in the CMDB. Ideally the tool used to move software into and out of the DSL should also simultaneously update the CMDB. Where this is not possible, procedures for accepting software into the DSL and for using software from the DSL for release building must check that a CMDB entry has been made prior to accepting or using the item. Where the SC&D and configuration management functions are combined, these activities can be carried out almost simultaneously. In-house developed software must have the necessary quality control documentation before it can be accepted into the DSL.

It is also necessary to back-up the contents of the DSL regularly to both local and remote storage areas. The frequency of such copying will be determined by the volatility of the contents of the DSL and its overall size. An option is to back-up the DSL whenever a change occurs to the contents, but this may not always be practical if there are frequent small changes.

Regular housekeeping of the DSL must be carried out. This will include regular reviews of the size of the DSL, to ensure that sufficient space exists for future versions of software. If there is a danger that DSL space may run out, more space must be made available, for example by increasing the size of the DSL. Software versions no longer required should be archived, and deleted from the DSL. Archive copies should themselves be deleted when no longer required.

5.1.2 Release building, distribution and implementation

The ongoing processes of building, distributing and implementing software must be carried out in accordance with the procedures planned and already described in section 3.1.

It is recommended that a post-implementation review is carried out, if practical, for each software release. Faults with the particular release should be put right; more importantly, faults with the SC&D procedures or tools should be put right to prevent any recurrence of problems.

5.1.3 Informing personnel

The Help Desk, computer operations, network control and problem management/specialist support staff must be kept informed of all software releases, and the Help Desk staff should pass all relevant information on to the users. Everyone should be made aware of any effects that the new release will have on them.

5.1.4 Configuration audits

SC&D staff should provide all necessary assistance to configuration management staff who will conduct regular configuration audits of the live/test environments and of the DSL against the CMDB.

These audits are needed to check that the software in these environments has not been deliberately or accidentally amended or corrupted.

The following points must be checked:

* are the versions in use the authorized ones?

* have the versions been amended in any way?

* have old versions been controlled to ensure that they cannot be deliberately or accidentally used?

These checks may prove particularly difficult or expensive in the case of large distributed systems. Consideration should be given to the use of automatic checks made by software, from the central SC&D node, of the software at all distributed nodes, perhaps as part of the system load procedures.

Regular independent checks by the organization's computer audit section should also be carried out.

As with all audits/reviews, configuration audits should be fully documented, management reports should be produced and any corrective actions identified must be followed up.

**5.1.5 Reviewing for
efficiency and effectiveness**

It is recommended that the SC&D function be periodically reviewed by IT Services management for efficiency and effectiveness, and that the results of the reviews should be documented and acted upon. Subsequent reviews should check for satisfactory progress on previous ones. Any changes that are recommended as a result of the reviews should be subject to normal change management procedures.

A review should be carried out shortly after the SC&D system is implemented, to ensure that the plans were carried out correctly and that the system is functioning as intended. Any problems detected should be traced back to source and corrected as soon as possible after implementation of the SC&D system.

Thereafter regular formal reviews should take place - at least every 6 months (the SC&D Manager should, however, continually assess the efficiency and effectiveness of the SC&D system).

At these regular reviews the SC&D Manager must take a forward look at likely SC&D workloads for say the next 18-24 months, and must make recommendations for IT and staff resources changes to deal with changing workloads. Factors that will influence the efficiency and effectiveness of the SC&D function must also be reviewed - for example the organization's release policy may need to be amended in the light of experience.

An efficient and effective SC&D system must show a clear indication of the following:

* releases built and implemented on schedule, and within budgeted resources (but care should be taken to isolate any problems that are outside the control or responsibility of SC&D, eg application development delays)

* very low (ideally no) incidence of releases having to be backed-out due to unacceptable errors (note however that software releases need not be entirely error free - a decision can be made to go ahead with a release despite the presence of errors, providing they are of a minor nature - see the **Problem Management** module)

* low incidence of build failures

* secure and accurate management of the DSL with no evidence of software in the DSL that has not passed quality checks

* no evidence of re-work on any software that was not extracted from the DSL

* DSL sizing matches demand for space, and timely and accurate housekeeping of the DSL is evident

* compliance with all legal restrictions relating to bought-in software

* accurate distribution of releases to all remote sites

* implementation of releases at all sites, including remote ones, on time

* no evidence of unauthorized reversion to previous versions at any site

* no evidence of use of unauthorized software at any site

* no evidence of payment of licence fees or wasted maintenance effort, for software that is not actually being used at any particular location

* no evidence of wasteful duplication in release building (eg multiple builds for remote sites, when copies of a single build would suffice)

* accurate and timely recording of all build, distribution and implementation activities within the CMDB

* a post-mortem is carried out on all release activities, and all necessary corrective or follow-up action is taken

* planned composition of releases matches with the actual composition (demonstrates good release planning)

* IT and human resources required by SC&D are subject to good ongoing forward planning.

5.1.6 Auditing for compliance

This sub-section is a checklist for those organizations that wish to audit their SC&D function (using the organization's computer audit section, which is independent of the IT Services section), for compliance to the procedures and advice in this module. It is recommended that an audit is completed at least annually; frequent audits may be needed initially or where particular problems are evident.

Configuration audits should be carried out as described in 5.1.4. In addition:

* change documentation (delivery notes, RFC records etc) pertaining to software placed in the DSL should be examined to ensure that only software that has been passed through quality control and authorized by change management has been allowed into the DSL

* all requests for software from the DSL for re-working must be examined to check that they have been correctly authorized

* maintenance activities on software should be checked to ensure that reworking is being done only on software from the DSL

* records of DSL maintenance should be checked to ensure it is being carried out in accordance with laid-down procedures

* records for the build, distribution and implementation of test and live software releases should be checked for completeness and accuracy

* for each release, the build, distribution and implementation records should be checked against the release record to verify that **all** the correct software versions, as authorized by change management - and **only** the correct software versions - have been included at all stages in the build, distribution and implementation of the release

* release records should be checked against the software actually used at all locations to ensure that they are in step

> * where applicable, the documentation for the live builds should be checked to verify that the live releases have been built separately and not just copied from the test environment
>
> * the documentation for periodic reviews of future SC&D staff and IT resources should be checked for completeness and accuracy
>
> * a check should be made that any problems with the SC&D system are traced back to source and put right within an a reasonable timescale (eg in accordance with problem management targets)
>
> * a check should be made that efficiency and effectiveness reviews are regularly carried out and that follow up activities are undertaken and then at a subsequent review, scrutinized.

Many of the checks described in 5.1.5 can also be regarded as 'compliance checks' - eg 'are software releases implemented, as authorized, at the remote sites and on time?'

The results of these audits should be documented and presented, probably in summary form, to IT Services Management. All the necessary follow-up actions should be identified and carried out. At subsequent audits, a check should be made that follow-up actions from previous audits have been carried out.

5.2 Dependencies

In addition to the dependencies listed in section 4.2, audit interrogation software is needed to identify inconsistencies between the CMDB, the DSL and the build and target environments, and to check that all actions have been carried out accurately and securely. Section 7 gives further details of required support tool facilities.

The organization's IT plans for the next 18-24 months must be available in sufficient detail to allow the SC&D function to plan its human and IT resource requirements reliably.

5.3 People

The key people involved in running the SC&D function are:

* the SC&D Manager and staff - who install quality controlled software into the DSL and who perform the software release build, distribution and implementation procedures

* the Change Manager - who is responsible for authorizing the timing and contents of the release, in conjunction with the SC&D Manager and the rest of the CAB

* application development staff - who deliver software to the SC&D team (via quality control) for inclusion in the DSL, and software maintainers (or developers employed on maintenance work) who request controlled items from the DSL for re-work as sanctioned by the Change Manager

* computer operations, network management and software testing personnel - who run or use the systems built and implemented by the SC&D team

* users - who may be involved in simple software implementation processes, though this is not recommended.

5.4 Timing

IT Services Management should formally review the SC&D system for efficiency and effectiveness shortly after implementation of the new procedures and at regular intervals, at least every 6 months, thereafter. These regular reviews should also update SC&D resource requirements for the next 18-24 months. The SC&D Manager should **continually** assess the efficiency and effectiveness of the SC&D system.

An independent audit of the SC&D function for compliance to the procedures and guidance contained in this module should be carried out at least annually.

6. Benefits, costs and possible problems

As organizations become more dependent on IT, the effective control and security of their computer software assumes greater importance. Organizations must be able to cope with a high frequency of software changes and development without sacrificing IT service quality. In many cases the software is to be used in several locations that are geographically dispersed, and such software must be controlled in an efficient and economic manner.

The guidance in this module helps organizations to achieve the necessary control.

6.1 Benefits

The principal benefits of an SC&D function, when combined with effective configuration management, change management and operational acceptance testing functions, are:

* the software in live use is of good quality, because software releases are built properly, from software that has been subject to quality control and effective testing, and under proper change management control

* software is released to the live environment in a way that minimizes the chance of error, eg by use of an incorrect version

* an organization's software assets, upon which the organization may be heavily dependent, are properly and securely safeguarded

* an ability to absorb high rates of change to the software on the live systems, effectively and without adversely affecting IT service quality - essential in today's IT environment

* the ability to build and control the software used at remote sites from a central location

* the ability to maintain consistent software over a large number of locations, which leads to financial saving because support is made easier and more economic

* reduced likelihood of there being illegal copies of software in use at any location

   *   easier detection of wrong versions and unauthorized copies of software

   *   reduced opportunities for unnoticed introduction of viruses or other malicious software.

As the efficiency and effectiveness of SC&D grows, the productivity of IT Services staff is likely to increase. More importantly, productivity benefits are likely to be realized amongst end-users. Even a modest assumption of a 0.5% increase in end-user productivity attributed to software quality improvement resulting from SC&D, would indicate large savings.

6.2 Costs

The costs associated with SC&D include:

   *   staff costs - please see section 3.3

   *   file storage costs - to accommodate the DSL, build environments, any additional test and live environments, and archive copies

   *   the cost of computer and network resources for moving software into and out of the DSL, and for building, distributing and implementing software releases

   *   the cost of software support tools (and the cost of any additional hardware needed to run these tools)

   *   initial time costs - for a short period it may take longer for changes to be implemented using the new SC&D system, but when staff become experienced the new procedures should take no longer, and may take less time, than the old methods.

In almost all cases the costs will be outweighed by the benefits. For example, many organizations cannot function satisfactorily unless they can handle a high incidence of software changes without sacrificing IT service quality: SC&D gives them that ability.

Without adequate control, organizations are at risk from such things as computer fraud, inadvertent software corruption, software viruses and other malicious software. The damage caused by these could cost an enormous sum to rectify.

6.3 Possible problems

The following problems may be experienced when initiating and running a SC&D function.

There may be some initial resistance from staff who are familiar with old procedures and who may not welcome change. To overcome this, the benefits of the new procedures must be carefully explained during the awareness campaign.

Circumvention of the SC&D procedures may be attempted. This needs to be dealt with firmly, particularly where unauthorized PC software is introduced into the organization as this is the most likely entry point for software viruses and other malicious software.

Circumvention of SC&D, change and configuration management procedures to make urgent fixes should also be banned as the dangers involved are too great.

There may be some reluctance to carry out a complete software build in the live environment instead of copying over software from the test environment. This is, however, essential unless the two environments are in every way identical - which is very unlikely.

In the case of distributed systems, difficulties may be caused if new versions of software are not brought into use on time or as required. This problem can be avoided if central control facilities, automated if possible, are used, backed up by regular configuration audits.

When the new procedures are implemented there may be a temptation to retrofit them, from the outset, to all software. This could be wasteful, and it is generally better to apply the procedures initially only to newly released software. At the point when the effort involved is considered justifiable - this is likely to occur only when the percentage of software not yet controlled under the new procedures is quite small (typically between 20% and 5%) - consideration should be given to retrofitting the new procedures to existing software.

Some people (including IT Management) may regard the SC&D procedures as cumbersome and expensive. Nevertheless, they are almost invariably necessary to cope efficiently and effectively with software changes.

7. Tools

Facilities are required to:

* create the DSL and restrict access to it

* maintain the DSL

* create and maintain build environments

* build releases from the DSL into test and live environments

* distribute releases to remote environments under central control

* implement the distributed releases

* verify that distributed releases are in use

* archive and delete superseded versions of software.

Most modern mainframe operating systems provide many of these facilities.

In addition, facilities are ideally required to document in a CMDB all authorized changes to the content, location and status of software and to carry out the changes under the control of configuration management, automatically updating the CMDB whenever software is transferred, distributed or implemented. For further information on configuration management support tool requirements, refer to section 7 of the **Configuration Management** module of the IT Infrastructure Library.

Where networks are being used to distribute software releases, facilities to control this distribution from a central control node are highly desirable. So too is some method of automatically passing back confirmation or relevant failure messages from each location to indicate if the release has been correctly received and then if it has been implemented.

Software tools are required for checking bought-in software, especially PC software, for viruses or malicious software.

Audit support tools, such as library matching or file matching facilities, are needed to check the integrity of the DSL and the live, test and build environments. Facilities are needed to check the live, test and build environment against the DSL; and the live, test and build environments and DSL against the CMDB.

When procuring and using support tools, the following
guidelines should be followed:

* tool requirements should be clearly specified to
  prospective suppliers

* all tools purchased should be adequately evaluated
  and tested before acceptance by the organization

* records must be maintained of acceptance tests and
  of subsequent reviews of the efficiency and
  effectiveness of software tools

* new software tools should be evaluated for
  compatibility with existing tools/utilities

* tools should be brought under the control of change
  management.

Annex A. Glossary of terms

Abbreviations used in this module

CAB	Change Advisory Board
CI	Configuration Item
CMDB	Configuration Management Database
DBMS	Database Management System
DSL	Definitive Software Library
IT	Information Technology
RFC	Request for Change
SC&D	Software Control & Distribution

Definitions

Baseline	A snapshot of the state of a CI and any component CIs, frozen at a point in time for a particular purpose.
Build environment	See **Live build environment** and **Test build environment**.
Change Record	A record containing details of which CIs are affected by an authorized change (planned or implemented) and how.
Configuration Item (CI)	A component of an IT infrastructure. CIs may vary widely in complexity, size and type - from an entire system (including all hardware, software and documentation) to a single module or a minor hardware component.
Configuration management	The process of identifying and defining the configuration items in a system, recording and reporting the status of CIs, and verifying the completeness and correctness of CIs.
Configuration Management Database (CMDB)	A database which contains details about the attributes and the history of each CI and details of the important relationships between CIs.
Definitive Software Library (DSL)	A secure software library where all versions of software configuration items (CIs) that have been accepted from the developer or supplier are held in their definitive, quality-controlled form (by necessity this logical library may have to occupy one or more physical locations).

Delta release	A release that does not replace all component CIs of a release unit, but rather includes only those CIs that have changed since the last version of the software.
Full release	A release that replaces all components of a release unit, regardless of whether or not they have changed since the last version of the software.
Live build environment	A computer system or discrete part of a computer system (made up of hardware and system software) which is used to build software releases for live use.
Live environment	A computer system or discrete part of a computer system (made up of hardware and system software) which is used to run software that is in live use, and sometimes to build software releases for live use.
Package release	A release that includes a package of software CIs that are introduced into the test, and subsequently the live, environment together.
Release	A software CI which is introduced into the test, and subsequently the live, environment. In most cases the release will also include documentation and possibly hardware as well.
Release record	A record containing details of which CIs are affected by a release (planned or implemented) and how.
Release unit	The 'level' or 'complexity' at which software of a given type, or a particular software item, is normally released into the test and live environments - for example, a full TP system; a suite; a program; a single module.
Request for Change	A form or screen, used to record details of a request for a change to any component of an IT infrastructure.
Test build environment	A computer system or discrete part of a computer system (made up of hardware and system software), which is used to build software releases for operational acceptance testing.
Test environment	A computer system or discrete part of a computer system (made up of hardware and system software), which is used to run, and sometimes to build, software releases for operational acceptance testing.

Annex B. Example job description - SC&D Manager

Main duties

1 Mounts publicity campaign to win support for new SC&D procedures.

2 Arranges recruitment and ensures training of staff.

3 Plans and implements the new release building, distribution and implementation procedures.

4 Plans and creates the DSL and build environments.

5 Evaluates and procures support tools.

6 Ensures correctness and completeness of DSL contents, by controlling all inputs, outputs and housekeeping.

7 Builds, distributes and, once tested, implements all software releases, as scheduled by the CAB.

8 Ensures that only authorized software is introduced into the test and live environment(s).

9 Assists configuration management staff to carry out configuration audits to check for the existence of unauthorized software in the build and target environments; arranges for the removal of offending items, and takes steps to prevent recurrence of any infringements.

10 Ensures that DSL, build and target environments and CMDB are always consistent.

11 Continually reviews the SC&D function for efficiency and effectiveness, and future requirements.

IT Infrastructure Library
Software Control & Distribution   Comments Sheet

CCTA hopes that you find this book both useful and interesting. We will welcome your comments and suggestions for improving it.
Please use this form or a photocopy, and continue on a further sheet if needed.

From: **re: 1992/SCD**

           Name

     Organization

        Address

      Telephone

COVERAGE
Does the material cover your needs?
If not, then what additional material would you like included.

CLARITY
Are there any points which are unclear?
If yes, please detail where and why.

ACCURACY
Please give details of any inaccuracies found.

If more space is required for these or other comments, please continue overleaf.

OTHER COMMENTS

Return to: **IT Infrastructure Management Services**
CCTA, HM Treasury
Gildengate House
Upper Green Lane
NORWICH, NR3 1DW

Further information

Further information on the contents of this module can be obtained from:

IT Infrastructure Management Services
CCTA
Gildengate House
Upper Green Lane
NORWICH
NR3 1DW

Telephone 0603 694855
(GTN 3014 - 4855).

The price of this publication has been set to make a contribution to the costs incurred by CCTA in preparing the copy.

Printed in the United Kingdom for HMSO
Dd296937 3/94 C5 G3397 10170